Condors

Written by Michèle Dufresne

PIONEER VALLEY EDUCATIONAL PRESS, INC.

Flap, flap, flap.
The black **condor**
went up, up, up.

California condors are one of the largest flying birds.

Condors have black **feathers.**

Condors have a red sack.

throat sack

A condor's bald head keeps rotting food from sticking to it. The skin on its head can change color to show how it is feeling.

bald head
wing
feet

The condor scans up and down. Can it see a snack? Yes! But it is not a plant.

Condors are a type of vulture. They eat dead animals. They mostly like big animals such as deer, cows, and sheep.

Condors do not like plants.

A condor does not trap or drag its **prey**.

Condors do not have talons, so they cannot grasp or carry prey with their feet.

Look up at the condor's **nest.**

Condors build nests high on cliff ledges and in cave openings and holes in tall trees.

glossary

condor

feathers

prey

nest